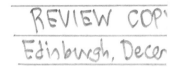

CW00689773

Nocturnes

David Olsen

Nocturnes

© David Olsen

First Edition 2021

David Olsen has asserted his authorship and given his permission to Dempsey & Windle for these poems to be published here.

Published by Dempsey & Windle
15 Rosetrees
Guildford
Surrey
GU1 2HS
UK
01483 571164
dempseyandwindle.com

British Library Cataloguing-in-Publication Data

A catalogue record for this book is available from the British Library

ISBN: 978-1-913329-48-8

Printed in the UK by Imprint Digital (Exeter)

With admiration and gratitude

Paul Surman
Hanne Busck-Nielsen
Dr Anne Hammond
Ellen MacDonald-Kramer
Carolyn Moseley

Also by David Olsen

Unfolding Origami
(Cinnamon Press 2015)

Past Imperfect
(Cinnamon Press 2019)

After Hopper & Lange
(Oversteps Books 2021)

Poetry chapbooks from US publishers include *Exit Wounds* (2017), *Sailing to Atlantis* (2013), *New World Elegies* (2011), and *Greatest Hits* (2001).

Acknowledgements

The following poems have appeared in the places cited:

Acumen: 'Interval or Final Curtain'.
Assent: 'Winter Worry'.
Cyclamens and Swords: 'Night Tremors'.
Exit Wounds (Finishing Line Press): 'Purgatory'; 'Trio'; 'Gelato'; 'Pole Star'; 'Embers'; 'Disorder'; 'Boutique'; 'Interval or Final Curtain'; 'The Farther Night'.
The French Literary Review: 'Beaujolais'; 'Say Cheese'; '*Night Café in the Place Lamartine*, 1888'; '*Starry Night*, 1889'; '*Le cœur de la France en feu*'.
Ink Sweat & Tears: 'Blue Light'.
London Journal of Fiction: 'Serenity in Dining'.
In the Voice of Trees, (Cinnamon Press competition anthology): 'Silver Birches'.
Poetry in the Plague Year, (The Poetry Kit): 'Woman Descending Stairs'.
Poetry Salzburg Review: 'Gelato'.
Sailing to Atlantis (Finishing Line Press): 'Winter Worry'.
The Vermont Literary Review: 'Lighthouse'.

Nocturnes was a semi-finalist in the 2020 Word Works Open Reading. Samplers from versions of this collection were highly commended in the 2014 Geoff Stevens Memorial Poetry Award competition of Indigo Dreams Publishing, and long-listed in the 2019 and 2020 Cinnamon Press Literature Prize competitions.

'Pygmalion's Marble' was long-listed in the 2018 Plough Prize competition.

Kate Waring's musical setting of 'Winter Worry' was performed at the University of Cambridge, England, by Jessica Lawrence-Hares in Fitzwilliam Museum and Clare Hall (2009), and in Churchill College (2013).

Contents

Nocturnes 2

V

Overture

Proud bottles muster, labels front;
stemware inverted overhead,
bottled beer in glass-fronted fridge,
tap handles poised for the first pull.
Booths are tidy, stools aligned.
The flat screen's mercifully silent,
awaiting a match on Sky.
No puddles on the gleaming zinc.

The barmaid brushes back a stray hair,
smooths her skinny jeans.
The barman checks the clock,
plucks a brass key from its peg,
crosses to the frosted glass,
unlocks the expectant day.

Nocturnes 1

In Music, a short composition of a romantic nature typically for piano. In art, a picture of a night scene.

Silver Birches

1.
Serrated yellow leaves
engrave evanescent names
into early snow.

2.
A century after the French
fled the searing breath
of General Winter,
sleigh runners glissando
through fresh crust.

Distant bells toll;
troika bells jingle
through ringing air.

Beneath crystal stars,
a young woman
wrapped in fur rugs
breathes blades, dreams
of white nights in June.

3.
An old woman's funeral.
Slavonic chants aspire
higher than bare birches.

General Winter, General Frost or General Snow
refers to the harsh winter climate of Russia.

Nightfall in the Taiga*

Night falls of its own weight;
the day shrugs to shed its burden
of schemes and cares.

The night slips in with gently
darkening stealth, as if shod
in felt boots.

Night is more than the absence
of daylight – a sensed presence
with its own latency.

The dark releases unseen stars
from cerulean confinement
to indigo liberty.

Wind through larch, spruce
and pine carries the howls
of lunar wolves.

Snowfall in the night
settles flakes of faceted
momentary sparks

coalescing in pearlescent drifts,
to embrace, perfect, and heal
the wounded earth.

* The swampy coniferous forest of high northern latitudes, especially that between the tundra and steppes of Siberia.

12

Verisimilitude

Beneath the proscenium the set appears real,
though the side walls meet the one at the rear
at oblique angles, and the mouldings are styrofoam
or papier mâché. Walls are so flimsy they tremble
when she slams the door.

And yet we accept the words, the emotional truth
conveyed by characters whose travails resonate.
Their cares become ours; we feel what they feel.
The entire performance approximates the reality
of the lies we tell ourselves.

---

* The appearance of being true or real

Becoming the Words

Anticipation is the worst part,
but none of this is about me;
I must be the humble servant
of an author who's entrusted
me with perfected words.

While waiting in the wings,
I tell myself to trust my lines,
trace the vein into their heart,
to give them spirit, breath, life.

I – having only an ephemeral voice,
whose tones will fade and still –
must bear the lights and speak
into the mouth of the dark,
and *become* the precious words.

V

Woman Descending Stairs
Île Saint-Louis, Paris
~ after Stéphane de Sakutin

Night enfolds
        her solitude
                in mystery's cloak.

Descending stone steps
        to the quai, she enters
                a street lamp's corona.

Her winter coat's
        pulled close against
                the atmosphere's weight.

Moss besieges cobbles
        on the landing, where
                a tree grows into shadow.

A second rank of stairs
        declines toward the Seine.
                Will she reverse and take it?

One wants to create
        a coherent narrative
                or purpose to the scene,

but none is apparent.
        No one else is in sight;
                her sole companion's the night.

Speaking of the Dark

The decisive struggle
occupies the shadows,
where obsessions roam
chiaroscuro regions
of subconscious thought.

And the evil in the heart
lurks in the wakeful night,
when grievances echo
through intense silence.

When a velvet curtain
at last descends, nightmares
become journeys across
a familiar yet strange sea,
where the terms of reality
are redefined, and questions
defy plausible replies.

Dreams depart at 3, leaving
the relief of deliverance.
Yet the quest for sleep remains
unresolved; the afflicted
fights the bed to no avail.

04:28

A disc of Max Richter's *Sleep*
ended hours ago. In a Rothko blur
between awake and asleep
I recall droplets of the dream:
on a strange street I meet
someone I recognize from …
I can't remember where.
I'm vaguely familiar to her, too,
though we can't recall names.
Her hair is light brown.
A simple floral print's
nipped in at her slender waist.

In my reverie,
four twenty-eight reverberates,
insistent as a hungry infant's cry.

Nearly awake now.
For the first time in months,
maybe years,
I think of Fiona, a petite
brunette with ice-blue eyes.
We were on a station platform.
She was earning a diploma,
so I rode in another carriage
to give her time to read.

I open my eyes
and turn toward the clock.

The LED reads 04:33.
The colon blinks
in time with my heart.

17

Blue Light

A pain in my leg wakes me at 4.
I stand to stretch out the cramp.
Blue light pulses on the ceiling.
I part the drapes. Across the street
an ambulance ticks. In a pool of light
from a street lamp, an old man
is trundled out, an oxygen mask
on his face. His wife follows in robe
and fuzzy pink slippers. They depart
in silence through the empty streets.

When I was small, my Mom told me
to say a prayer whenever I see
an ambulance, or hear its siren.
I return to bed, thoughts flashing.
Unable to sleep, I try the World Service
and Shipping Forecast. Something
reminds me of Mont Saint-Michel
and how the narrow causeway floods
when the rising tide rushes in
faster than a man can run.

Serenity in Dining

I wear a fine bespoke suit and greet
the regulars with a confident smile,
remembering their likes and dislikes,
including their preference for water –
sparkling, still, or iced – the choice
confirmed by unobtrusive hand
signals to the assistant server.

From a memorized list, my sommelier
is ready with suggestions to match
selections from the evening's menu;
he's unfazed whether the chosen wine
is moderate or extravagant in price.

When the duck arrives on the *guéridon*,
I carve one breast with the right hand,
the other with the left, to avoid
rotating the bird and exposing
its unappealing cavity to the guest.

Three or four hours later, I supply
complimentary cognac with a bill
of four figures, while maintaining
absolute poise, never revealing
my thoughts to the people I serve.

Sommelier : a wine waiter

Boutique Window, Night

A haven in a dark market street,
the spotlit display seems a refuge
of warm companionship

and comfort imputed to light,
like the glow of a lone watchman's
cigarette or the constant polar star.

In a silent conspiracy of elegance,
three faceless mannequins dressed
in the season's coloured frocks

harmonize like improbably slender
sisters whose rivalries are past,
their present accommodation

an alliance bound by shared
history and blood, united against
those outside the plate glass.

Two Nocturnes
~ after James Abbott McNeill Whistler (1834-1903)

1. *Nocturne in Black and Gold:*
The Falling Rocket, 1875

Dying stars from skyrockets embroider
the charcoal-grey night, enlightening clouds
of roiling smoke above Cremorne Gardens
near Chelsea. Two indistinct figures
on the near bank of the Thames are vague
translucent squiggles of unrealized
afterthoughts of spirits not quite there.

2. *The Lagoon, Venice:*
Nocturne in Blue and Gold, 1879-80
(after the bankrupt painter's flight into exile)

The muted blue lagoon is enclosed by
blue-grey clouds and charcoal silhouettes
of a square-rigged ship and a tower rising
from distant structures emitting points
of golden light. Foreground depicts
three gondolas seemingly aground in grey.

Night Café in the Place Lamartine, 1888
~ after Vincent van Gogh (1853-90)

Stars, blooming in summer profusion,
punctuate a scroll of indigo sky.
Light from tall windows emanates
from dark façades down the street.

Newcomers emerge from the shadows
of the cobbled avenue to join diners
and drinkers at white tables outside
the all-night café – for night people,
those too skint to pay for lodgings,
or too drunk for admittance elsewhere.

Burnt-orange and sunflower-yellow
gaslight warms the scene, welcoming
the artist without homeland or family
nearby. In a letter to Theo, Vincent
asserts an improving sureness of touch
and intensity of concentration.

V

Starry Night, 1889
~ after Vincent van Gogh (1853-1890)

The dominant cypress seems a flame
mirrored in a church spire rising above
a slumbering village and olive grove.

The calm on the ground contrasts
with the painter's sleepless distress –
his restless mind revealed

in the swirling turbulence
of a riotous indigo sky's fierce
eddies and sweeping currents.

Yellow-green ripples amplify
the crescent moon and stars
burning with raw fire.

Siege at Night
~ *after Jonathan Ernst, Reuters*

Blurry silhouettes loom against
unruly clouds of teargas and smoke.
Amid the clamour and cries

a steed bearing the bronze
Andrew Jackson rears up,
as if spurred by rage or fright.

In the middle ground, helmets glisten
on both sides of a new steel fence.
Beyond the barrier, the pendant lamp

in the White House's North Portico –
meant to welcome visitors – is barely
visible through the fog of battle.

The People have made the connection
between a Minneapolis murder by police
and a bully occupying the People's House.

Not far away, soldiers prevent access
to the Lincoln Memorial, the capital's
symbol of enduring aspirations for justice.

Rivers of humanity flood distant streets
to expose lingering inbred bigotry,
a deadly virus in urgent need of cure.

Lighthouse

In welcome and warning,
probing fingers palpate
the organs of the night.

The patient resistance
of this obelisk of grief,
this pedestal of care,

is its only triumph
over the persistent
riderless horse.

***Freedom from Fear*, 1943**
~ after Norman Rockwell (1894-1978)

Two sleeping children share a bed
in a darkened upstairs room. Mother
bends at the waist to adjust a crisp
white sheet. Father, their guardian
in white shirt and light-grey slacks,
stands by, reading glasses and newspaper –
with headlines of war – in his left hand.

Somewhere, with cruel indifference,
bombs fall on dark Stygian cities.
Curtained homes are aflame;
fire hoses writhe in rubbled streets;
people, choking on ash and smoke,
shudder on cold concrete platforms
of tube stations, unable to sleep.
But not here. Not in the warm home
of Rockwell's American Everyman.

V

St. Louis, Missouri

Amid the flashes of fireflies
on humid summer nights,
in those days you could walk
a residential street, and every house
had open windows, with screens
in place to keep out mosquitoes.
To let out the heat of the day,
front doors were open, too,
with screen doors the only proof
against the onslaught of bites.
Yet some people would sit
on the porch with a Bud,
slapping bugs and rolling a cool
bottle across a hot forehead.

From every front room
came the sound of a radio
tuned to the Cardinals game.
You could walk the length
of the street without missing
a single pitch: balls and strikes,
fouls and base hits. Cheers
for the home team's home run.
And Stan the Man on his way
to yet another .300 season.

Chiaroscuro

Chiaroscuro in art, is the use of strong contrasts between light and dark, usually bold contrasts affecting a whole composition. the treatment of light and shade in drawing and painting.

Echo in C# Minor

I meant to sing my life in C major,
according to a sprightly Mozart score,
with playful improvisations
and plentiful grace notes –

a song with variations on a theme
conveying a sense of progression
toward a satisfying journey's end
at the resolved tonic C.

But as intentions inscribed in the lines
of the left palm are realized on the right,
a life as lived diverges from the plan.
Destiny's a smirking illusion.

The echo of my song returns, transposed
to C-sharp minor. Its mood is more sombre
while accounting for wound and grief.
My simple song is becoming an aria

blending comic and tragic parts,
whose harmonies and discords
are complex and enriching threads
of interwoven light and dark.

Driftwood
Redwood Highway, California

Cool winds and overcast skies bar sunbathers
from the white sands of this lonely stretch of beach.
Bleached like desert bone, driftwood from beyond
the blade horizon has come to rest as if weary
from a journey of exile and rejection.

A plank with lignin ridges and chamfered edges
lies in a tangle of seaweed and strips of kelp.
Branches stripped of bark are scattered about,
and grandpa sees one that seems a snake;
another resembles the bill of a duck.

He picks them up, trudges resistant sand
back to the car. For a reason known only
to the moment, this detritus from the sea
seems a gift to be taken home, there
to languish among rounded beach stones
that have dried and lost their lustre.

Beach Walk

Sun on sequined sea. Renoir clouds
blown by wind of Beaufort 3. Gulls soar
above the cliff on an updraft, the lift of pure
unburdened air enabling some, like waves,
to become a stasis of constant change.

Collars closed against the chill,
we're indivisible atoms of eternity,
unmeasured and timeless,
seeking a dimensionless truth
behind the screen of metaphor,

suspecting that the symbol is itself
an invention without meaning,
a conceit like a grain of sand
tossed in turbulent surf, confined
in approximate place by groynes.

Our familiarity secure, you and I
no longer take snaps of each other
in such a scene. Assured of only
this moment, we trust a retinal spark
to retrieve this sliver of infinite space.

Sea Glass

A sandy strand littered with broken shells,
uprooted kelp, driftwood, and smooth stones
that will lose their lustre when they dry.
Flies crawl over the fractured carapace
of a dismembered crab. Amid the detritus
a piece of sea glass glints – not pure flint
glass, but grey-green from iron-rich sand.
Its concavity suggests it might be a bit
of side and bottom of a six-ounce Coke
bottle from the wartime '40s. Shallow pits
frost the surface after a prolonged tumble
in pounding surf, and abrading encounters
with countless grains of sand. If I rescue
this eroded gem from its fate of reversion
to particles of sand, it would be an intrusion.
In some form, this gift will survive me.
With a resolute fling, I return it to the sea.

Lyme Regis

Its hunger insatiable, the tide
gnaws at the Jurassic undercliff
with the patience of a life force
without limit or expiration.

Seawater spoons grains of earth
soft as sugar, reveals coiled
ammonites buried when
memory was planetary.

The precipice edges back.
Homes surrender gardens;
dead ends of streets recoil
as wire barriers shift inland.

Black bones exposed by leaf-fall
engrave a zinc plate of sky
as roots scrabble to grip friable
earth as it slowly cascades

to be ingested by a sea rising
from indifference or neglect.

Blur

The scene is a Rothko;
    there are no sharp edges.

Everything's indefinite,
    as if viewed from the fog
    of a half-waking dream

in which each coalescent
    droplet casts its shadow.

You might see
    only dull grey, but in truth
    there is a cuvée of greys

subtly balanced
    with a winemaker's skill.

The gorse is grey-green,
    the grass a shade away,
    a distant oak still another.

The ridge is greyed ochre,
    but the granite outcrop nearby

blends quartz, mica and feldspar
    to aggregate
    crystallized sky.

Redwoods in Rain
Northern California coast

Sunlight shafts would,
in fair weather, slant
through cathedral groves
like a god's commands.
Without apology,

a storm brewed
in the Gulf of Alaska's
cauldron blunders in,
an unwelcome guest:
clumsy and drunk.

Zinc-grey nimbus
is barely visible
through a canopy
woven into a design
too dense to comprehend.

Rain drips from needles
to oxalis on the forest floor,
soft and spongy underfoot.
Chocolate streaks stain
fluted bark of tannin red.

Young trees sprout from the hulk
of a fallen log sustaining moss,
shelf fungus, and lichens,
deserving the name
Sequoia sempervirens.

Boardwalk
Devastated Area, Hawaii

I'm treading a boardwalk
across undulating ground
paved with rubble:
black volcanic bombs.

The sole instance of life
is a bare blackened tree
lacking twigs or leaves.
The sun's behind a notch
between two limbs.

I stop down to f/16;
in the print a scintilla
of sun will yield
a six-pointed star.

The silhouette is stark,
as if from a stage set,
as if waiting for Lucky,
Vladimir, and Estragon.

Witness for the Defence
Redwood grove, California

A cross-cut slab of redwood round,
a foot thick and yards across,
tilts against a granite boulder.
Certain annual rings are marked:

1914
    1776
        1492
            1066

With the patient wisdom of stillness,
these old-growth trees have witnessed
a millennium of climate stasis –
centuries of seasons, similar
but not identical, as if time were
a tweed with subtly varied threads.

Cold upwelling from depth cools moist
Pacific air; fog coalesces on needles
and drips to the forest floor to nurture
shallow roots spreading, intertwining
like fingers clasped underground
in secret sisterhood.

Adapted to these benign conditions,
and with fireproof bark, redwoods lack
a taproot, are vulnerable to change.
Violent gales and torrential rains prise roots
from softened soil. Venerable trees fall.
If survivors of fire and chainsaw could speak,
what would they say to reckless neglect?

That Maple

The walls in the upstairs bathroom were blue,
but in the season of New England's glory,
they shone burnished gold from copper leaves
on the maple just outside the window frame.

Instead of heralding the looming end of the year –
when homes fold in upon themselves, and drivers
grit their teeth to skitter down the taut season's
gritted roads – that maple marked the climax

when wood was chopped and sawn and stacked
for warming a second time, and neighbours
prepared for when solitude and reflection in tight
houses became the apotheosis of primal home.

Window screens were taken down; the leaf rake
stood in reproach while awaiting expiration
of a game clock; the mower growled through
the season's last cut. Despite the calendar's

firm assertion that the year begins in January,
autumn seemed the true beginning: the school year
in clothes chosen to allow one to grow into them,
and teachers viewed with trepidation or awe.

Friendships were renewed and new ones forged
in hormonal fires. Even now, while I brush
my teeth amid the golden glow of memories
of youth and renewal, that maple recalls all.

Stubble in Snow

A few miles south of here,
the Wyoming prairie
got no early-winter snow
from the recent flurries,
but here, where it's just
that much colder, stalks
of hardy grass penetrate
a light dusting of pristine,
untracked white. They
twitch in gusting wind –
thrust and counterthrust –
but persist in resilience
rooted in possibility.

Whiskers on Earth's face
will outlast deluded men
claiming ownership where
weather, water, and soil
welcome windblown
immigrants held in trust.

April Snow

April demands forbearance.

It should be spring.
You deserve spring.
By now the taut season
should be a memory,
as ashes on the hearth
recall the fire.

As if to prove the point:
bare maples are trying to bud;
aspens, arising like skeletal ghosts
from nowhere, strain to birth leaves.

In the glazed stream there is stirring.
In snow tunnels there is scurrying.

But a rogue nor'easter,
perversely late,
plucks feathers from a zinc sky.
Wet and clinging, they clog
wheel wells of cars
skidding through slush
too soon black.

Pines kneel in submission,
dip weighted boughs.
In supplication you await
the turning of calendar leaves,
scrape the heavy shovel on the drive,
try to emulate the resigned
and patient snow.

Bright Angel Trail

A thousand feet
    above me
        from the red-rock
           canyon rim
               like a line
                    casting for trout
                        a filament
                  glints in sun
              curves in wind
          spinneret's
       sibilance
    a melodic line
      a hymn
          in silk

So Be It

Beneath a cerulean dome,
fescues nod their obeisance
in the supplicating expanse
of a flower-dotted field.

An orphaned, childless oak
drowses in solitary dotage
like a retiring priest who wearies
of mumbling seasonal liturgies.

Far from apparent kin or source –
seemingly without parents
or progeny – this tree must seem
a god to the genuflecting grass

whose wavering gaze must
have missed the acorn lost
by a clumsy jay preoccupied
with trim and pitch and roll,

or a forgetful squirrel
whose autumnal industry
invested unwittingly
in a harvest of perennial plenty.

On the wind's a Druid's chant
rejoicing that this sacred tree's
not surrendered to the vanities
of a handsome chair or writing desk.

Gelato

Embraced in the cotton wool
of Florentine summer warmth,
we lust for bracelets and rings
in Ponte Vecchio's emporia,
emerge into broiling sun,
then retreat into the shade
of a strategic *gelateria*,
where smooth alpine slopes
glisten with gemstone colours.

I choose double chocolate,
but you ponder with slow
greed all flavours and hues,
tasting each with your eyes,
deciding at last on pale green.

We lean on the parapet above
a single scull's patient skim
along the green Arno's skin.
Beyond are terra cotta domes
atop tiers of honeyed stone.
You offer your cone for a lick;
we share cool, sweet relief.
Pistachio.

Beaujolais

A coach tour north from Lyon.
She and I have left behind cafés
shaded by awnings and planes
beside the Saône and Rhône.

Beyond Villefranche-sur-Saône
few are on the village streets.
Heat that swells and sweetens
Gamay drives everyone indoors.

a variety of grape / Gamay wine a light-bodied red wine

We pass *vignerons'* stucco homes
painted in local earth tones:
yellow and darker ochre.
Weathered wooden shutters
cover windows, blocking all light.

CA, USA.

I recall summers of my youth
in the Diablo Valley.
My folks captured morning cool:
shut windows, closed blinds,
drew drapes against the sun
until evening brought relief.

I imagine what it would be like
to live in places we visit.
Idly, I tell her if we lived here,
we, too, would spend summer days
in darkened rooms.
                    She thinks
of summers by a northern lake:
No, we wouldn't.
Under my breath,
more thought than sound:
Yes, we would.

44

Say Cheese

I want to capture you
    as you view the Loire
        from the bridge.

Let's preserve this sunset moment,
    after drinking a local red
        and strolling the town,

arm in arm –
    our bond loose,
        yet secure.

The shutter clicks.
    I trust the image
        will have fidelity

to the original,
    and delude myself
        with its permanence.

The goddess

is a long twisted wire
                    of stellar aspiration

a line curling
                into 3-
                        dimensional

                space

a wilful
                    unpredictable

        consciousness

a minor triad
                    resolved

to a single
                sustained

                    unrepentant tone

        and I am the plinth

V

Pygmalion's Marble

The cool block of Carrara exuded possibility.
She was in there, somewhere, a seductive pose
awaiting release with stoical patience
he was unable to summon in himself.

He whispered to her while his ardour grew.
White chips flew in their dozens and scores,
fell to the studio floor to form a white beach.

Boutique

Neither shapely figure nor skin –
perfect, smooth, and pale –
arrests my eye.

It's the gown of elegant cut
in a subtle swirl of jewel hues:
violet, indigo, cerise.

Your colours –
those *you* possess
as if created just for you.

Oh, how you would look
in that fetching dress
with your long slim line

this mannequin
is meant to represent,
while failing the ideal.

Even on the High Street
of a city you've left,
I still window-shop,

browsing here and there,
seeing you everywhere.

Entropy[1]

Ignition began
when a corneal spark
set alight the tinder of desire.

Slow combustion
consumed the entirety
of all that was.

At a random moment
smokeless burning cooled
until a final burst

of perfecting flame
yielded spirit-smoke
and a sifted residue –

grey-green ash
scattered by indifferent heirs
resentfully clearing clutter.

Rain shifted the ashes by inches;
wind dispersed them further,
first this way, then that.

[1] A scientific concept as well as a measurable physical property that is most commonly associated with a state of disorder, randomness or uncertainty.

Tuesdays in the Café

Every first and third Tuesday
the blond American
meets friends at a table for six.

He arrives early,
when the place is quiet,
orders Earl Grey.

He lingers at the counter,
pays over the going rate,
just to be nice.

He walks with me
while I take the tea
to his usual seat.

At Christmas he gave me
a card with a fiver; that day
his tea was on the house.

He seems to like
my black hair pulled back,
my eastern European accent.

Does he think
I'm too young for him?
Or he's too old for me?

When I serve his friends,
his gaze follows me.
Moist eyes reveal thirst.

Seeking Ginny Weasley

Dawn's dew of possibility
evaporates in the desiccating
breath of meridian sun.

In quest of an oasis –
a refuge from desert heat
in the eye of the sky –

the Wanderer exceeds
the dune's angle of repose,
slips as helpless grains slip.

The hapless Wanderer
slides into a depression;
efforts to regain the heights,

or even equilibrium,
are repelled by
cascading infinite sand.

The onslaught is relentless,
brutal foes too numerous
to overcome with futile toil.

Shadows lengthen until
the unintelligible night falls,
and still there is no relief.

The Wanderer searches
for purchase on sleep –
the comfort of the unconscious –

then come illegible dreams.

Nocturnes 2

Ghost

The memory lingers, cool in air,
then disappears like a faint star
when I attempt a closer look;
winking like a sequin obscured
by a shifting fold of satin;
a liquid spilling, at once revealed
and concealed in a penumbral
shadow of half-light.

She's an echo in minor key,
music with undefined tune
sung by a spirit, perhaps
a figment, the workings
of an overwrought mind
haunted by the shadow
cast by a willing illusion.

Not light, but lightness.
Not presence, but absence.
A persistent scent or
                         something

here, there, everywhere –
always and never.

Winter Worry

Rain crystallizes
jewels on my dark
discontented pane.

Hissing cars
slither through
the terrible night;

their headlights
gloss the meaning
of the slick

serpentine road,
that Möbius strip
of this lover's hope,

this coward's dread.
From the shaded room
the glass reflects

a ghostly troubled tread,
as I await
the cabochons

of your eyes,
the mother-of-pearl
rainbow in your smile.

Night Tremors

I know I'm keeping you awake;
I hear the stifled sigh as patience
erodes to faulted bedrock.
It's just an ankle's twitch –
as when my flipper foot
taps the pedal to keep
a coughing engine running –
but it's enough to quake
the bed and break the silver
threads in the web of sleep.

I explain that the micro-fit
is beyond conscious control;
it starts in a primitive part
of the brain, and excites
motor neurons ruined years
before the Salk or Sabin
vaccines came on the scene.

None of this helps. There's
a paroxysm of doubt when
I worry if this is just the first
of those petty annoyances
that may, one day, shake your
forbearance with seismic force.

Trio

Unable to sleep, we try music.
Once a romantic dinner companion,
sprightly strings of Schubert's B-Flat trio
fail to soothe, and instead annoy.
Up for melatonin. Down to try again.
You try to read, can't concentrate.
I wait for exhaustion to overtake
the ache of mind. Today was the day
for you to say you've *met someone*.
Will this piece be forever ruined,
destined to become Our Song?

Continental Drift

An unsuspected fault splits
Pangaea. The tectonic rift rends
a whole whose parts survive,
diminished and adrift.
                    Dreams
subduct into an oceanic trench.
Rough edges of shelf conform
like spooning lovers reconciled.

Pole Star

Two stars
          in close orbit

rotate round
          a common centre,

oblivious
          to others

as if the universe
          is of no concern.

But long
          exposure reveals

their curving trace
          is one of many;

only the Pole Star defines
          the fixed centre point.

Its constancy guides
          those who've gone astray

in moments
          of madness.

Purgatory

We arrive separately
    to a meeting we always
        attended as a couple.

You sit next to me;
    we fumble a brief squeeze
        of hands under the table.

Others pretend disinterest,
    try to behave as if
        nothing has changed.

The urge to stroke your back,
    to rest my hand on your thigh,
        as before, is irresistible.

You turn to me,
    and fix an intense gaze
        on my eyes, and smile.

This is no passing glance.
    Your eyes condemn me
        to a lingering limbo,

a purgatory of ambiguity.

Disorder

The removal men have left,
their raucous voices gone; the scent
of their sweat and smoke dissipates.
At last the house is entirely hers.

Where paintings and prints once hung,
bare picture hooks stare from walls
where un-faded paint leaves void
rectangles of aching vacancy.

Cutlery drawers are in disarray.
Detritus of packing paper
and spent spools of parcel tape
litter the floors in every room.

Where his furniture has gone,
there are depressions in the carpets.
Replacements must be ordered,
tardy delivery men awaited.

A few indivisible items, bought
together in hope, remain;
others were carted away
to an address she'll never see.

What remains is the husk of a house
renovated in eight months of weary,
but joyful, weekends spent
building a home together.

The phone rings. The Other Man
calls from his home abroad:
Well done.
Now you are free.

The half-empty house fills
for an hour: promises are made;
obsession's quenched. She will await
the next call or text. Night falls.

Interval or Final Curtain

Was that the last act,
or the end of the first?

The plot seems unresolved –
too many loose ends,
too many possibilities
for corrosive unfinished business.

People in black shift a bed,
move hands on the clock,
flip calendar pages,
place a wine bottle just so.

The players (a goddess;
a comic sidekick;
and a leading man,
less than gentleman,
more than shadow)
fidget in the wings,
uncertain whether to wait
for the safety curtain to rise,
or take off makeup
and put on winter coats.

Someone
should tell the players
if there's more to come.

Embers

Embers glow
    with faint intent.

Shall they be stirred
    to renewed warmth,

or shall they fade
    to cold indifference?

Might our tragedy –
    worthy of Puccini –

be resolved by waking
    from a nightmare of deceit?

And would the will exist
    to heal our wounds?

Black Dog

The black dog
answers to any name,
comes whether called or not,

tongue lolling,
nails clicking
across a hardwood floor.

The black dog requires no care;
it feeds itself,
needs no visits to the vet.

The black dog
never wags its tail,
wakes at the worst time.

The black dog's nose
unerringly sniffs out
the most vulnerable.

The black dog is master,
chooses its own time
of leaving.

V

A magnolia bedsit

of static familiars:
December memories
frozen on the dresser,
guitar with slack strings,
incomplete crosswords,
remaindered paperbacks
glowering in silent reproach,
a clock's numerals glowing red.

Outside the window, a stylus
engraves the sky's ennui:
a few people going somewhere.
Entropy of dispersing contrails
reveals a tiring universe
winding down to stillness.

Another day in limbo.
Another lonely night
of indeterminate length.

Eurydice

Even now, I can't resist looking back.

Object of a satyr, in quest of escape
from the quotidian, the goddess
was doomed by a viper's bite.

She fell under the predator's spell,
was taken to a dark place of no return –
a place of which I know little,

and comprehend still less. I bargained
for her return, but every plea failed.
Her monstrous fall haunts me still.

The loss is overwhelming, the grief
so intense, that it seems fatal for me
to peer into the irreversible dark.

Le cœur de la France en feu
~ *Paris Match*, 15 April 2019

Ending months of silence,
after a wounding assault

on a *Parisien*'s heart,
you send a note to lament:

Notre-Dame is our *cathedral.*
I reply with memories shared:

Futile attempts to capture perfect
rose windows and sanctified sun.

In the shadow of her bell towers,
quick kisses on a *bateau mouche.*

In an oasis of light on Île St-Louis,
moules and a carafe of merlot.

Our moonlit crossing of Pont St-Louis
to stroll round the cathedral's east end,

its flying buttresses like ribs
embracing an eternal heart.

The Farther Night

In daylight I see no more
than ninety-three million miles –
eight light-minutes.

But if, in my solitude,
I wander into a clear night,
I see beyond the retired sun:

Saturn as an evening star;
Betelgeuse and Sirius;
the spangled Milky Way;

the chalky smudge
of a Magellanic Cloud;
the faint glow of galaxies

and nebulae – so far away
that their current events
occurred millions of years ago.

Just as I see farther at night
than in the day, in the dark
tones of a solo tenor sax

your face is there,
a constant constellation
in the velvet night.

Penumbra

However I try to illuminate
an abyss of tenebris, to force
light into corners of grief,
I avert defeat only to the extent
that wrestling with the dark
yields an inevitable stand-off
between equal adversaries
who grapple and draw apart,
weary and out of breath, each
regarding the other with distrust,
our struggle unresolved.

Survival depends on becoming
resigned to inhabiting shadows,
accepting rules of engagement
imposed in the semi-dark
night of the blood moon.

Notes

Two Nocturnes: Whistler began his suite of nocturnes, originally titled *Clair de Lune*, in 1871. Many were based on visual memory, rather than immediate observation, and could be interpreted as dream landscapes depicting atmospheric moods of the Thames in and near London. Whistler painted *The Lagoon, Venice* while working on commissioned etchings of Venice, after bankruptcy forced the loss of his London house and the distressed auction of several paintings.

***Night Café in the Place Lamartine*, 1888** and ***Starry Night,* 1889**: These paintings by Vincent van Gogh appear in the present order to contrast the artist's evolving state of mind near the end of his life. In the former, the artist is confident; in the latter, he is in turmoil.

Siege at Night: This poem describes a documentary photograph of a public protest outside the White House in the aftermath of the 2020 murder of George Floyd by a Minneapolis police officer.

Freedom from Fear is one of four paintings inspired by President Franklin Delano Roosevelt's 1941 State of the Union address, informally known as the Four Freedoms speech. Norman Rockwell supported the war effort with paintings for the *Saturday Evening Post*, each representing one of the freedoms enumerated by Roosevelt. Millions of poster reproductions were distributed. The original paintings adorn four compass points of the central rotunda of the Norman Rockwell Museum in Stockbridge, Massachusetts.

St Louis, Missouri: Stan "the Man" Musial played for the St. Louis Cardinals National League baseball team, and carried a .300 batting average through each of 18 consecutive seasons.

Seeking Ginny Weasley refers to one of boy wizard Harry Potter's loyal friends.

Le cœur de la France en feu: The roof and steeple of Notre-Dame Cathedral in Paris caught fire during the early evening of April 15, 2019. The title of the poem is taken from the cover of a special edition of *Paris Match* magazine. The title could be variously translated as "The Heart of France Aflame" or "The Heart of France on Fire".

A poet and playwright with a BA in chemistry from University of California-Berkeley and an MA in creative writing from San Francisco State University, David was formerly an energy economist, management consultant, and performing arts critic. He has lived in Oxford, England, since 2002.

See www.davidolsenpoetry.net.